Emotions

Dipika G. Murty

ISBN 978-93-5610-536-2

Published in India 2022 by Pencil

A brand of
One Point Six Technologies Pvt. Ltd.
123, Building J2, Shram Seva Premises,
Wadala Truck Terminal, Wadala (E)
Mumbai 400037, Maharashtra, INDIA
E connect@thepencilapp.com
W www.thepencilapp.com

Author biography

About the Author:

Dipika Gongala Murty is a professional sportswoman, an ardent reader and a keen observer. She believes that beauty lies in small details and in the emotions attached to each. This reflects in her poems too which are inspired by true incidences of life and emotions as were felt!

CONTENTS

Acknowledgements

I am grateful to God for this life and all the treasures therein…my parents, my Sir, my family and my friends. A heartfelt thanks to every single soul and every single moment that has bestowed me with the most beautiful gift of ….. Emotions!

A special thanks to…

Yaisna Chingshubam & Yohaan Remedios for their creative contributions.

Enjoy Reading!

THE GIRL WHO GAVE

Giving is Divine!

In the circus of life, you were born to suffer

To breathe in strife, to grow in litter.

In the circus of life, you look so dingy
Your merest touch makes all cringy.

In the circus of life, you seem shallow,
Waiting to grab with no morals to follow.

Yet, in the circus of life, you earn every bread
Not a full-grown, you are a contorting child instead.

In the circus of life though you lay at a fall,
When you shared your penny, you made everything small!

And in the same circus of life, you will one day, outshine
Your sparkling kind eyes will brighten up, every ravine,

And in the same circus of life, though you were born to suffer,
You will be a Golden Star and be blessed forever!

HIDDEN CHILD

Live as the beautiful child in you!

In the name of savoir faire, stands
Every body spruced up and staid.
Shimmering in envious attire,
Every gesture well rehearsed is displayed.

But to splash in muddy puddles
Every inner child still craves.
Failing to veil with dirt smudged faces
Is the mirth of mischievous forays!

In the name of etiquettes, dines
Every body in fine cuisine.
Manoeuvring manners into every morsel,
And beguiling in a performed routine.

But to relish with hands full,
Every inner child wishes to gorge.
Licking corners of wrappers and fingers,
Only in pure merriment does hunger submerge.

In the name of sociability, utters
Every body an impressive word.
Flattery is laden with pretence, for
No genuineness can a business afford!

But to vent all true feelings
Every inner child yearns to scream
Silly, wise, right, wrong… no judgement binds,
Feuds lay buried & amity reigns supreme.

Can we just, in no way give up
How unique we are meant to be
And can we not just, revel in everything
As the beautiful child in you and in me?

SMILING EYES

Wear a smile always!

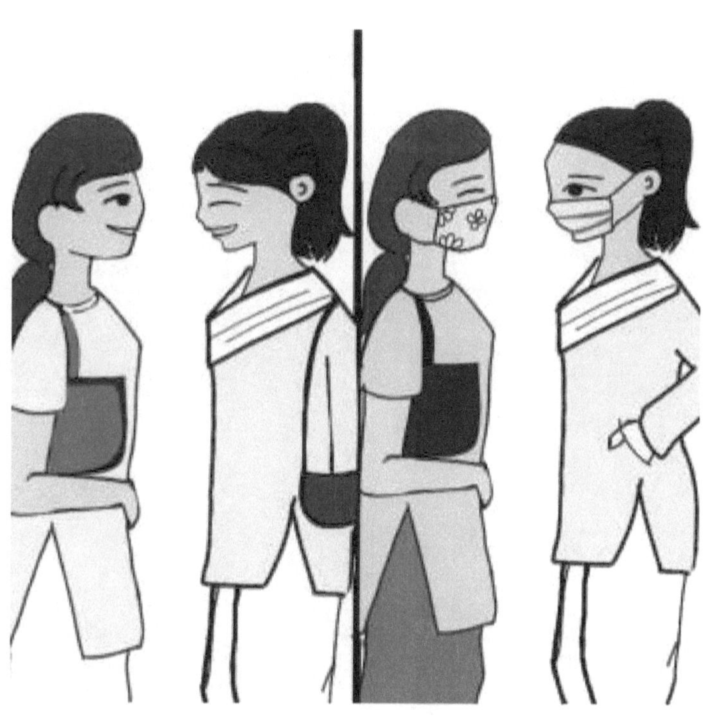

Emotions

As smiles drip saline into my soul,
Seeking them, always, an ever undaunting goal.

With barriers now shielding every countenance,
The trading of smiles is forbidden, hence.

How my soul grapples to withhold its grace.
Searching the contours of every masked face.

And when some gazes I deeply beheld
It dawned on me that thoughts can gel.

My soul now tears every mask that lies
Salinating from your smiling eyes!

EQUAL

Respect and accept every being!

I am softer subtler prettier
Heaven chose to make me so
I am a part of the perfect creation
How can u say I am less or low?

If you are in need you worship my form
Yet swearing on my name is such a norm
If you are insecure you seek my comfort
Yet defiling my body is never an effort.

I am the light, so spirited and bright
I have wings of hope and skies to conquer
But what makes you demark and shorten my flight
And what fun you get to see me flicker ?

Aren't we here to complete each other
Not to suppress but raise the other
Why can't you understand, when this is so simple
I and you are different but will always be EQUAL!

THE DEVIL

Connect to souls not phones!

Was there a time...
When living was so free,
When souls lay bare over cups of tea,
When dampened lids had shoulders to wet,
And when bouts of laughter balmed every regret?

Was there a time...
When shared glimpses pulsated every vibe,
When a touch rocketed sensations inside,
When chastity embellished every trait, and
When togetherness shone with pride innate?

Was there a time...
When the smile of a beloved bestowed content profound,
When strangers got befriended without inhibitions abound,
When faith lay saddled on every prayer
When morals were nurtured layer by layer?

Now is a time...
When living is so confined,
When souls smother in dark ravines,
When tears are sold and so eagerly bought,
When laughter, only to appease is sought.

Now is a time...

When the double lensed eyes only lust

When devoured with malice is every bottom and bust,

When carnal desires shroud all sanity,

When aloofness and privacy bask in vanity.

Now is a time...

When entwined with the Devil, is every mean mind,

When no surroundings matter, no acquaintances to find,

When with doubt and fear every life is chained,

When the Devil... the Damn Phone depletes all scruples ingrained!

FREEDOM FIGHTERS

A gift to preserve!

Anger and anguish all inside,
Waiting to unleash was every cry.
Born into enslaved India,
Our life was but a quest to survive.

With Birth, came our very Right,
To flourish and prosper on our motherland.
Yet nothing was within reach...
Dreams were crushed at a stranger's hands.

NO!! This will not go on
Determined and fierce grew every mind.
'We shall arise, awake and stop not
Till the goal of Freedom, we find!'

And then the greatest of valour displayed.
Proudly we martyred with shrouds adorned
Whether hung, beaten or burnt alive,
Yet, to die, new crowds were formed!

No Power could such bravery stand
At last our Tricolour swayed up high
Our lands our waters our winds were free
And we, the Freedom Fighters said goodbye...

But,

Oh...our countrymen born in Free India

May you learn from our sacrificed lives

To preserve our beloved motherland by,

Doing your Duties before claiming your Rights!

LOTUS FEET

Solace at your feet....alone!

When horizon lived next door,
Touching the stars, mere a chore.
When inhibitions could never hound,
Adolescent dreams saw no bound.

With luscious passion, each day I'd greet
Oblivious to the Grace of thy lotus feet!

Stumbling and struggling, stood up strong,
Proud with notion, nothing could go wrong.

No hurdle could stop, no storm could sway,
There was the Will, there had to be a way.
Dissolved in the maneuvers of the game,
Naive to the carpentry of thy Purple frame!

Longing for the emblem to rest on my heart,
Tearful pleadings, of every night were a part.
Before the ravines were ready to gorge
Thou chose the time for the alliance to forge.

Into my sweating body thou breezed
Arousing faith, every doubt thou creased.
Everything since is a journey of love.
Game, Life .. all in thy heavenly cove.

When I fall, I know thou will raise,
When I rise, I see thy smiling face.

O Conjurer, let me not any more illusions meet,
Just keep me tethered to thy Lotus feet!

LIFE

Bless all who come your way!

Saddled upon you every journey embarks,
Through plateaus of pride and ditches of doubt,
Through peaks of glory and plains of contention,
Heading to an obvious yet unknown destination.

And though with wails every ride begins,
Illusion bewitches the remainder of the way.
"All I desire I must acquire, and
The journey must smoothly thus transpire!"

And then begins the saga of hurt egos
Of regret and blame, hatred and revenge
Bathed in resentment, lay slumped on your back
With no reins to hold, all energy is slack.

But the equine Life has rules intact.
From the puddles of vice shall only, virtue emerge,
From the dirt of untruth shall only, truth reign
And from the depths of evil shall only, goodness shine!

So O soul, don't weigh with bitterness, but gallop light,
With grace and gratitude towards everyone,
Who on this journey has been placed perfectly,
For you to become the best you can be!

ALL YOURS

Nothing but you allure me, my Krishna!

Emotions

The breeze caresses my face,
Brushes my hair.. whispers in my ears,
Slowly and softly...
You are the one, my dear you are the one!

The flowers bright and lovely,
Secretly wink at me,
Breathe us in, they say.. for
You are the one, my dear you are the one!

The river sparkles in the sun,
Enticing, attracting, pulling me towards her.
When I ask her ..why? She giggles...
You are the one, my dear you are the one!

The handsome blue sky charms me all day,
Hires the shining stars to woo me all night,
When I pause and look up.. he grins...
You are the one, my dear you are the one!

They all know and yet they try...
I'll not be theirs this time.
For my heart is consumed by the One..
Who made them all for me to Smile!

MY CYCLE RIDE

Cycling is pure bliss!

I am riding with the breeze
To find new ways and cross new streets.
The trees are dancing along the sides
Showing me the way which is wise!

Pedalling across as in wonderland
I explore the world with different eyes
Some are rich, some are poor
Yet each one lovely and unique for sure.

And then some guys just swish past me
Grinning as they overtook me
But you all just wait and watch
As I chase so swift so fast.

Besides the challenge and fun of race
The beauty of life comes face to face
You ride on your journey, I ride on mine
Together we shall meet even if for a while!

My cycle my friend ..you carry my weight
Of my body and my mind as well.
Just a little ride on you
Makes me lighten and fresh as dew!

POTTER

Hollow without you, my Sir!

In total dismay was a lump of clay,

When an aperture of hope came its way.

The glory of those moulding hands

Pulled the lump like magnetic strands.

Once the Master crafted his wheel
The clay was blessed, its fate was sealed
Every flaw smoothened with diligent grace
The lump soon acquired, a silhouetted face.

The great zealot left no stone unturned
In the kiln of hard work every ounce he burned.
The shimmering urn was lauded on many lands,
Yet had its haven, under the creator's hands .

On the day of lights, the Potter said goodbye.
Shed the weight for his soul to fly.
And since, the shadows are not to be seen
In total dismay, I, the urn have been.

O come back ...my Master
O come back to me
For a lump of clay in your hands
Is all I want to be.. ..

"I shall be with you forever, oh urn,"
A voice from heaven said in turn.
"Impart all that you have learnt from me
A lump of clay is not what you are meant to be .."

THE LOOK .....TEXTBOOK

O Mummy, you are the best teacher!

On The flame of prayers
Simmer delicacies of love.
And when my burps grace the meals
A look of pure contentment unveils.

Broken glasses or strewn wears
Every mess dealt with deligence
And when my naughtiness seem to might
A look of stern warning shoots upright.

In tumultuous times or criticism,
Calmness silently prevails.
And when my confidence is shaken to the core
A look of absolute faith braces more.

Come feats, applauds and rewards,
In gratitude head bows, hands join
And when pride begins to seep in me
A look pierces, for grounded to be.

Never a look of pity nor a look of arrogance,
Never a look of pretence nor a look of weakness.

But you only give me what you want me to imbibe.
O my Mother.. your every look is the textbook of my life
!

GUESS WHO

The lifeline!

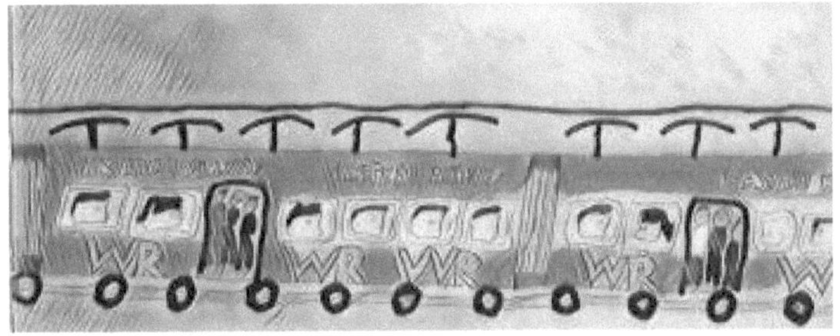

With grace compared to none,
You swarm out before the sun.
And so enslaved by your domineering sway,
Are the changing moods of the day!

Flirtatious is your presence
And alluring is your cadence.
No wonder, millions swoon over you.
Unmesmerized? Hardly a few!

The sheer potency you exhibit,
Gives every nerve a twist.
So swift, so sleek and so agile
Toting lustrous dreams all the while.

No matter how many pound upon
In elegance you move along
You garner faith unbelievable
You are no less than a miracle!

Why are all so fondly smitten?
Who is this tantalizing one ?

Oh! No one can from you refrain...
You are .. The quintessential ..Mumbai Local Train!

THE FIRST PLAYGROUND

Let me be your friend for life!

In the playground safely enveloped
You aped swings and frolicked a lot
Summersaulted and tugged for attention
And in shared excitement, I wobbled inside out.

Wailing a red wiggly bundle then appeared
Clearly missing his merry go round.
And in pure content soaked my every atom
Seeing the cute monkey in human form !

Naughty eyes always searched for me
Tiny fingers poked and pulled
Little arms and legs frantically inviting
To be clad in an embrace, we both so longed.

Crawling, you hid in nooks and corners

Tumbled, wailed and started all over.
Keeping a vigil on your whereabouts
Sun, moon and stars even existed? I doubt.

O my Bunny, now as you become taller
You'll play new games and have new friends
But do not forget your first playground, for
In those memories your mumma will wobble life long.

RAISE YOUR VOICE

Every step starts with you!

With her first wail, forsaken or auctioned for sale
Shut not, those rebelling eyes but forcefully raise your voice..

When she is ready to leap and stride, with pseudo morals she is tied.
Don't hesitate to rationalize but strongly raise your voice..

When she longs for a book but is admonished to cook
Let the world criticize but proudly raise your voice...

When she is teased and raped and also unabashedly blamed,
Don't let condolences suffice but vehemently raise your voice.

When she soars past the masculine she is belittled and judged
Shun the demeaning noise and boldly raise your voice.

While she slogs for the family, aspersions are cast on her readily
Don't wait for the worst to arise but firmly raise your voice.

www.ingramcontent.com/pod-product-compliance
Lightning Source LLC
LaVergne TN
LVHW050427160726
843469LV00041B/1268

9789356105362